GET FRESH BOOKS

In *throttlebody,* the life of the mouth is primary: My body counts on the sound of water in the mouth... These wholly original poems slip through time with wild sensual metaphor, from the Camaro bucket seat to the visceral life of the tiny fan, the Hemi Cuda; from the top/bottom lip to the bird-shaped birds to fish swimming inside the body. Alexander talks to the dead, who breathe in lines of stunning imagination— these poems are fuel-injected, running hot, alive.

—Jan Beatty, author of *The Body Wars,*
University of Pittsburgh Press

I'm excited to tell you about how good Lisa Alexander's poems are, and what a welcome breath of fresh air her book, *throttlebody* brings to contemporary American poetry. These poems are smart, funny, insightful, sexy as hell for the way they sizzle with sensuous detail, and they have that rare ability to draw us into surprising, other realms. The poet understands the way that domesticity can be beautiful if you look closely enough, and her clear-headed and unsentimental take on the working class, including the literal and figurative landscapes of that world feels personal. In fact, the emotional range of the poems is inclusive, even sometimes painfully so. I love this book. I hope you'll read it.

—Bruce Weigl, author of *On the Shores of Welcome Home,*
winner of the Isabella Gardner Poetry Award

THROTTLEBODY

Poems

Lisa Alexander

Get Fresh Publishing, A Non-Profit Corp.
PO Box 901,
Union, NJ 07083

www.gfbpublishing.org

ISBN: 9798218357672

Library of Congress Control Number: 2024935571

Cover art: Liz Nichtberger

typesetting/design:
culture glut llc
cultureglut.com

This book was typeset in Bembo Std and Vtks Money 2.

For Joey

TABLE OF CONTENTS

iris, the mechanic

you sit around
with your head on
& look out the window to watch whatever
is falling from the sky & hope
whatever song plays next
is one you can take off on—
the sun, you know,
is at your eyes—
you see it instead
with your brain, your iris,
the mechanic, parceling
light into your pupils,
& doesn't this sound
familiar? Or is that just
hope again talking itself
into thinking some sense
can be found somewhere
to soothe the general
state of unhinge
that persists no matter
how hard you slam the door,
or even close it gently
like a responsible person—
still it slips ajar allowing light
to angle across your face
even when you close your eyes
to avoid it & dip into something
quieter & perhaps less

sonically loud—but this iris,
the mechanic, formed
within your sockets without you
even thinking about it,
& it serves you by allowing
infinite & impossibly old
movement inside your face—
for a time, anyway.

one

the soul is a canary sent
Into the mines
—Larry Levis

red dot

       mark of birth
on my head   little railroad-
riding graffiti guy tagged
me on my way out
of my mother   used to be
a half-dollar wine mark
crowning under my hair

mom points it out
in a video we once made
in case I ever went missing
       & someone had to identify my body
It's here—pointing down on the small crown
above my forehead solid finger poke
felt like she could touch my brain
that finger-in-the-belly-button
      deep heebie-jeebie

it's possible I came out of her
      red dot first:
the color of the uh-oh
     a searchlight

Looking for Johnny

At the C&L grocery, avoiding the ham-handed paper-hat
heads behind the deli counter, I slip to the frozen meat
section, kneel down to the grate mounted on the front.
Caked with gray fuzz clouds, it blows cold air from darkness
within. Peering into it like a periscope,

smooth little forehead pressed to its grit, I whisper
Johnny Johnny, the name of my cousin who died months ago.
His KISS posters scared me, but I loved
his black '77 Chevy Cargo van with the red-carpeted
interior. I am four, and I believe he hears me when I call.

At the bowling alley with Grandpa, I eye the darkness
behind the pins standing at the end of the glossy maple
wood lane looking to find him there: *Johnny Johnny*

At home, crouching in the dimly lit laundry room, I call for him
inside the tall green furnace, searching through the metal slats,
    saying his name to the center of the blue flame.

I've Got Walls for Days

Blustery afternoon, and I am nailed
to the picnic table. A small tag
with my proper identification tied around my neck.

Wind blows and I flutter.
There is nothing about that bird that doesn't
sound like a rusty swing set. Wind blows and I flutter.

Limbs flapping on some cold fall day
near the playground. "Bells for Her"
playing in and around my head. The sky hush with travel.

Domenic Whipped a Palm-

sized plastic football at me,
so I hit him across the face
with a sloppy fist.
Punching someone seemed
like a good idea until almost-impact.
My fist slowed, didn't want to fly full force.
He shoved me two-handed
into barberry bushes, and quick-to-get-up,
I grabbed his face with my right hand,
dug jagged nails in on his cheekbone,
in next to his mouth,
in above each eyebrow,
in above his nose.
Wincing, shouting, he smacked my arm down.
Yia Yia stomped onto the porch,
weakly shaking hot dogs in hand, teeth clenched,
yelling a mixture of angry, disappointed, tired, sick—
Stamáta! Élla thó!
We stopped, followed her into the house,
knelt quietly on the matted carpet
in front of the old Motorola.
Yia Yia hovered over the sink,
hacking and spitting into a paper towel.
Domenic, wet-eyed and sweaty,
five red half-moons on his face,
chomped his hot dog, staring at *McHale's Navy*
and I sat, paper plate untouched, digging rolls of skin
out from underneath bent nails.

Small, Stained Mouths

Wide-hipped fruit lies in a thin sigh of grass, speckled
with black spots I am afraid to eat.

Each pear a pouch dented from the push mower peddling
across the lawn that morning, slicing the skin,

little cut ovals left to brown like small, stained mouths
opening up all over the lawn. Collecting them

in my Frisbee with the four o'clock flower seeds
that look like tiny grenades, I throw bombs around the yard

all day, barefoot, making explosive noises
with my tongue and teeth, then taking cover.

From the chipped porch steps, Grandpa whistles for my cache, sits
in his web-strapped aluminum lawn chair. Knuckling a knob

or two from my plate, he cuts the pears with a six-inch knife,
feeds me slices clean from the blade.

apart the train

I'd run onto some tracks   to stop a train
    to get on a train   to take apart a train
throw it into the sky   the clouds mixing
    sunny-eye bleary-eye brightness
wasn't even heavy   that train went up
like nothing   I'd run the tracks
   skipping across   the rails stubbing
never feeling it   train never fell
        it just kept going up   so high
heavy warmth and fullness—so full and warm
I could feel it   miles away as I ran through
        the trees   stealth, giddy

Me & Becca in the Backseat, Leoma at the Wheel

She shut the headlights as we cruised in pitch
blackness, no moon, and I was scared, you know,
but not willing to admit it. Leoma herself
was an ignition, my best friend's older sister
with huge black hair like exhaust burning
above her leather collar. I love the depth
of a bucket seat, and her 1980 Camaro was magic
in their garage lit by long overhead bulbs,
but on this ride my eyes stretched for light
somewhere along this back road, hoping
like hell we wouldn't crash, and you know
she laughed at us in the rearview, two shady heads

trying to be tough, fingernails digging
hairpin curves into vinyl seats, pushing our thighs into the seams.

The Plum Tree

If you've ever led a strand of children
across a busy road to get them away
from your dead grandmother, you'd know
that one will always lag at the end of the line,
stare at the ambulance behind you.

Two of them will fight.
The brothers will shove each other
into the door of the KFC, creating a scene
for the customers who all saw you coming,
red–lit halos swirling behind your heads.

You're not really old enough
for this kind of charge.
Not that you want to be.
Your short arms are still reaching
out the upstairs window
for deep purple plums
from the highest branches,
while she holds you tightly around the waist.

tiny rotating fan

this tiny silver fan----*two-speed rotary*----
blows its skinny clippers----*a reeling whir*----
right out the small crack
                in the window [I lifted]
                to make room for some seepage::
                        ----*adjustable tilt head*----

and really I must seep [even]
                        if only a little to allow
                        for my own evaporation
                        over a never even
                                amount of time::

I could say something about needing
                [the space] but really I wouldn't know
                a gradual release
                ----*the window, the oscillating shadow fan*----
                if I met one some
                        rained-on/ dashed-out /sicko Sunday::

It's never until after I've left
                        the window cracked all night
                        ----*chill sheets marbling*----
                        & I've chattered a few bites
                        into my pillow
                        I'll realize there's been an escape::

two

Burning Rubber

This girl I thought I loved
gave me all of her Xanax
to help me deal with her bad days.
She drove us way out farm roads
to the tight winding, the selfish darkness.
She really could've dumped me
off a back-road bridge. Could've slit
my nipple, she bit so hard pushing me
back into the passenger seat.
I had to take the wheel so she could
stop driving me away.

Drunk Cousins Loud & Hanging

around the basement bar at Aunt Cecilia's
with bellies full of seven fishes & ouzo.
Boys who know what kind
of hide & seeker I am,
what kind of fighter, what life
at Yia Yia's house was like, what I've looked like
at 5, 9, 12, 17, 21, 25, 30, 35—
Nicholas, mouth stuffed with paximathia, says:
You know they have a gay group at Ambridge High now?
You believe that shit?
Everyone antes up & I'm engulfed: *fags, homos, sickos*
& Tino, in a pink popped-collar shirt is chanting
Gay Bash! Gay Bash! Gay Bash!
No one here knows my cat's name or how
I got the scars on my thumb, or what I do every day
or why I haven't brought a boy around since '98.
I want to say:
Remember when we played guns & you guys
all had girlfriends to rescue?
Remember I offered to have one
to make things easier, so I'd blend better?
Well, I liked it.
Instead, I swallow my ouzo hard.
Let it sting without a chaser.

BF Jones and My Mother

have nothing in common, do they?
Smooth marble steps, the statue
of Jones bronzed and stalwart in the library entrance.
Franklin Avenue cold in the winter
even when there was ice cream nearby, maybe
there still is, but back then it was more popsicle
stick mangers and Elmer's glue in the basement,
the construction paper heavy and dull,
       but oh, the rubber grip scissor slice.
       Oh, the *shuppa chup chup* of cutting a halo
for the Virgin Mary, biting my lip,
and my mother, Maria herself, tempered
by her dark brown hair, snapping her Trident gum,
holding the vast sheet for me as I cut,
my socked feet slipping through the backs
of the big wooden chairs. I cut more circles,
glue more wood, as my mother holds the apex together,
peels the glue from my fingertips,
with my prints, now see-through, swirling on it.

No Better

The young kid who lives next door
just called his dog a faggot.
His voice is about to change. I can hear it on
the cusp of deepening. I wince,
think *I am a faggot.* I like his dog.
I imagine a different version
of me, the one who goes to his porch, asks
him not to say that, although I know
it's likely the word of choice for a 9th grader.
Another version of me
goes onto his porch and
cracks him in the mouth
backhanded, tells him
not to be ignorant. I imagine him
at the same junior high I was miserable in,
at the lockers near the gym, boys slapping each other,
saying things to say them. His dog is fluffy
and golden, licks me when I go to my car. The kid has
helped me shovel snow, always says hi,
much nicer than his miserable sister. Maybe his
dog is a homo, who knows,
but I know when he said *faggot* he meant
asshole or *motherfucker* just as I mean
asshole or *motherfucker* when I yell from
inside my car at the butt fucker who cuts
me off.

Tin Cup Dog

Tin cup dog swings his brushy tail
back and forth along the flat cold
floor, sweeping up dust with his wiry
copper fur. Dinner was good last night:
burgers in red wine vinaigrette.
I'll take it any day, but I won't take
the other bad news—bad news today,
those dogs, I don't want to look. Don't want
to know any of it. I'd rather keep my eyes
on the A-line skirt and candy lips of this soft woman
or maybe even this endless, endless rain.

A Night's Worth

Standing on the street in
Gramercy after a night's
worth of walking across Brooklyn,
of hi-ball glasses smashed
in the street and kisses
from the androgynous supersexypunk
in the bathroom of the bar where
the floor lights up with beats,
hard, ass-thumping, rib-pumping,
bass-that-sucks-your-sweat beats.
A night built for fleeing and
we did. Left the car curbside
at the hydrant, but we were hungry,
really hungry, and lost the keys when the Japanese
woman yelled *Don't touch my pussy!*
and threw her broom but missed and we ran
to catch a sunrise of train ride
returning us to the city. We teetered
and reeked the whole way.
8 a.m. in Gramercy
the sun feels like the sun does after a night's worth
of walking across Brooklyn: amplified, magnetic.

Fog Off

I hear Edward say *America is a haunted place,*
and I feel haunted. Don't you? Not haunted
in that devilwentdowntopsychokillakilla way,
but occupied, or at the very least,
shot-through-with-scared-as-fuck.
We each lived on the inside
of someone else's body
for nearly a year, stacked
between someone else's organs, steeped in
the timbre of someone else's voice. We heft trunks
from the stream, scrape, grunt & breathe—

clouds sprout from our mouths, fog off
                    into the rank-streaked mist.

Snowmelt Road

I want to go to Ambridge
with Dad, in the bare brume
of musk cologne; the dark

blue Saturday nights, sit
on the perforated blue seats
of his 1984 Ford Ranger,

pens and tools clacking
in a cup under the dash.
I want it to be overcast,

dirty snow lining Route 65.
The last of the mills puff
into the gray wet grit

from spare pillars that jut
between rusted pale blue bridges.
I want to see my breath

while white ice clings to rocks
along the hillside striping
the muddy river. There's nothing

to hear except the shush of tires
along the snowmelt road.
Maybe a train will burn by.

We'll go to auto shops, art stores,
smell oil & rubber, the sting
of paint, rub my hands

on something greasy, wipe it
on my pants. We'll eat eggs & bacon
in the Maple Diner,

put jelly on our toast. We can pick up
whatever Manny or Larry or Gus
has for him: rolled up banners

or cardboard tubes capped
by plastic discs. I want to
wait in the truck, click
all his pens. Scrunch the vinyl
steering wheel, pull & plug
the silver door lock & read

Someday Angeline for the 30th time—
breathe on the window,
write my name in the fog.

Scoring the Sunlit Halves & Thirds

"I'm a Man"
by Spencer Davis Group
comes on the radio,
& my Greek father says:
I was at the Party Club
in Kaiserslautern, Germany,
when this song came out.
All the Germans went crazy.

In it the rolling organ
racks a rhythm
against the basement wall
that all the neighbors can hear,
I'm sure. That song
so unlike my mother, her smooth jazz
kept in the cabinet under the TV,
slips into the air on Saturday afternoons
roasting with baked chicken & potatoes,
scoring the sunlit lemon-dust particles
in halves & thirds, in blurs that drift
& will sink as the sun sinks, as the pointed
wide-yellow stare of the streetlamp
takes over.

Evacuate My Brain

Pegasus Club, Pittsburgh, 1996–1999

Along that wall
I could be quiet
in the dark—
club kids, drag queens,
brush by in a stiff hit
of hairspray, cigarettes,
something candysweet—
honey bring it close to my lips
I'd stand there smoking,
watch the crowd on the floor
move as a whole, look for faces
I know, faces that surprise me,
faces I might want—
honey bring it close to my lips yeah
the irresistible pull of flashing
colors, fog blur/bucket bass—
hot jungle *call on me—spin spin sugar*
electric *crawl on me—spin spin sugar*
spun us all down to sweat/skin
gathering everywhere, grinding
whoever was closest
twist on me—spin spin sugar
barely room to move—go ahead
let the roof lift off
this basement bar on Liberty
let those streetlamps shine right in—

Animal Bent

Seeds in the sycamore. Only a few left
up there anyway & they dangle
in a way that makes me feel filthy, not hungry,
even though I should be, but the vodka I drank
last night still swims in my body, making my dreams
all about work, worry too heavy, making me want
to run like an animal bent on getting away, crouched
in a ready pose, joints primed, escape like a cheetah
running so fast the ground is a blur below her.
    I dreamt I did this once, running first as a person—
    slow/stunted, then as danger got closer, I bent
    on all limbs & took off down a Beechview alley,
    leaping over high bushes, landing in the yard where I lived,
        darkness coming down like a garage door around me,
        the old house with her tall white stare,
        grass wet against my nose, it was a relief,
        finally, some kind of relief.

three

Tennessee Bourbon

I wanna get knee-walking
          drunk
     with Dolly Parton
     on her front porch,

                    stagger over to Barbara Mandrell's
                         house
                    to flash our moonlit tits,
                    howling, from her shrubs

Back of the Neck Excitement

Back of the neck excitement surges through me
at the mere mention of Blue Ridge Mountains, which,
like me, contain a massive range of tiny-belled desires,
like taste buds racked in salty brine
washed over by the thickest chocolate cake. How?
　　　How could I have possibly been both Naomi Watts
and a young man who was hiding
the fact that years ago he shot Jeff Bridges
with a very small gun in the middle of the night
in Hopewell Township, Pennsylvania?
But I was.
I was also the high school classes they both took,
and I was the memory in the boy's mind
hoping not to be discovered.
　　　Dreams like this are vents.
　　　My body counts on the sound of water
　　　in the mouth, the brush of lips
　　　grazing the phone receiver
　　　to be reminded that it is more echo than matter.
　　　It counts on quick breaths taken when you're
　　　impossibly close to someone else
　　　and they breathe back in response.

Whattaya Gonna Do?

I'll never have that ham sandwich again,
because Tarquinio Bakery went out of business
and the Virginia baked is not the same
since C&L turned into Shop n' Save
and Grandpa died. The cat I drew
on a place mat is still in the house,
probably in the dining room cabinet. Sometimes
when the sun shines right in my eye I hear a plane
and think of everyone who's given me something.
I have more than I say I do. I want more than I say I do,
but mostly what I want is to sit in his windshield-cracked Dodge,
click of the blinker so tight I feel it in my throat,
and let the jingle of the rosary dangling on the rearview
go on without ever once touching it.

On Boggs Avenue

Nikki Watroba is a friend
of the girlfriend of the girl
I've been making out with.

She lives downstairs & tells me about
the man who lumbers up from the basement
to sit on her couch to talk.
He's a Confederate soldier, she tells me.
He *is* her, she says, her past life.
I nod & listen
but don't go into the basement again.

Upstairs the junkies fuck loudly,
the burnt Bic-pen crack scent
drifts through my kitchen, but they
always say hi, offer me lunch.

I use a wrench to turn on the cold water.
The ceiling keeps collapsing in the corner.
Landlord doesn't care, so I paint
four wall-sized goddesses around
my tiny living room
after dropping acid one night.

Out front someone paints
PUKE ON LUCY
in bright green & purple
across five sidewalk squares.
I see it from my window
as daylight sinks over oak trees
on Green Tree Hill.

Lake Total Lust

I first saw her thick lips
across many heads
between us in a bar.
I wanted to lie
down in the crease
between her full upper
and her thicker lower.
Voice a steel ball rolling
through a pinball machine
& I was drunk on her for months.
Michael & Joey said
she looked around
the room too much,
they didn't trust her
when she called me to come
into her room with her boyfriend.
She's dragged you
along for a year, Joey said—
& now wants this?
In bed she kissed her boy's
dry lips before he
put them on mine.
She kissed me (finally),
& he could've fallen through
the floor (I would've preferred)
because I didn't want ready
dick, but I wanted a taste

of her enough to cheat
on my new girlfriend,
who was good to me
so far.
But they wanted
the lesbian show,
the how-hot-would-that-be
experience & I had
a dam in my chest
holding back the Great Lakes
of Misperception: Lake Total Lust,
Lake Blind Love, Lake Experimental Girl.
There was one alone moment
when he stepped out,
both of us naked—
I played with her
eraser-nub nipples
under the off-white sheets,
city summer through the windows,
& pretended
he was the 54C
rumbling down Forbes Avenue,
hissing his way out of earshot.

Jesus Christ Birds

Seven hundred thousand or so
chattering away in the yellow tree
taller than my neighbor's old-ass mansion.
The racket so manic,
I nebby-neighbor my head
out the window in my men's department
robe & yell *Jesus Christ birds!*
& it doesn't matter.
These are bird-shaped-birds,
little arrow shadows, bitching up a ruckus,
ticking like gravelly rockets,
crackling like the moment
before the Rolling Stones come out, just
as the lights go down,
arena crowd loud.

Stripper Karaoke Every Tuesday.
One Dollar Well Drinks.

The keyhole-shaped girl is emphatically singing
Scorpions' "Wind of Change" into a mic she holds like a hand job.
Three of us agree the bar smells like a roller rink rug,
& your boyfriend slides off to see someone he knows. I pry
my bourbon & your beer from the sticky fake wood
& return to you smirking along the wall. I smirk back.
We drink silently, snickering like jerks together.

You don't know what to do with another girl,
but you should tell your boyfriend to go home.
Not because he's in the bathroom snorting coke
with the stripper from Rikki Lake,
but because your tired eyes strike sexy,
& that groove in your cheek makes me thirst.

I Would've Been Sent Away

I still try to see behind the swings through the trees
by the power lines, I've been back there with Mike and Nick,
smoking, bullshitting
        before Mike went to jail and Nick
        closed the garage and turned the car on
I still have Mike's silver Swatch—hasn't run since '91
and yeah, I pulled that shotgun on Nick
        from my bedroom window after his big talk
        about his guns, I wanted to scare him away
These days I would've been sent away, made the *Times,*
        At the station, cops told me everyone knew Nick
        was a bad kid and I was a good kid so they let me go
I told them the gun was a toy, and they all believed it (except
for Nick and my dad, who locked up his guns from then on)
I haven't been behind the swings since then
        down the quad tracks
        that curve through woods past the playground
where as a kid I won a stuffed bunny
when my paper plate had a sticker on the bottom
and I was marked

four

Smashing the Inch

My raised bare foot
stepped and rammed
its littlest toe into a corner
smashing the inch of it again
for the countless time,
and I brought God into it, yelling
about senselessness, demanding
to know why I have pinky toes
if their only purpose seems
not to be balance, but little reminders
there's meaningless pain
around every corner.

Off That Day

Like I'm supposed to say
something about it,
how the last part of your body
I ever saw was the back
of your curly head
walking out the front door on Evaline Street
and I was pissed
because you took the good product
the only product that would tame
my hair even the slightest bit
and you died with it, that tube
of Rusk, likely kicked aside
by paramedics when they stretched
your body through that trailer
and out into fall sun.
Your hair was likely perfect,
chocolate-sprung ringlets shaking
as they racked the stretcher
into the ambulance.
You probably wouldn't have liked it,
always so critical of your hair,
just as you wouldn't have liked your viewing,
when I started smoking again, your Dad
lighting my first one back,
the fucking pastor
talking about how much he loves
Starbucks, the job you hated,
all of us who loved you

crammed into the side room, rolling eyes
over this preacher
who never knew you, your face
in that coffin stretched, as if you were repulsed
by this bullshit and your hair was off that day, frizzy,
and you wouldn't have liked it, and I would've
cut all mine off, if it would've made a difference, but
instead, I never used that product again.

Night on Rattlesnake Hill

Shelter should be here. Three miles in
and still a slim footpath, dimmer and dimmer

under the canopy. Our only light the size
of my finger when you stop at the marker

that tells us we've been going the wrong way.
The flatness of some states makes me nervous, wide

spans of too much information, too much space around
my body, not like this state,

the foresty-steepness of Pennsylvania
that curves possibility behind massive rocks. Potential mountain

lions perch overhead, bears spying me clumsily push
my way through weeds with food on my back, listening to me

talk loudly about orgasms and clit-on-clit sex to distract myself
from the thoughts that I, too, can quickly be eaten as it turns dark.

Three miles back we're whipped
by branches. Fall once, opening my knee, push on,

like walking midnight alone through a bitched up
neighborhood followed by three drunk men hollering.

We don't look back, or too far ahead.
We move on hope we haven't lost the path—

total darkness—the little light useless until we find a clearing,
pitch the tent, huddle together, your hot mouth

perfect darkness, naked for the first time.
We can't see snakes around us, although days later we hear

about the huge den just feet away from our tent. Made me wonder
who was sleeping next to us, one flap of rip-stop nylon

separating us from a curled-up muscle of poison.

Crocuses, Baby

for Michelle

means winter grit
is crumbling, gray icebergs
chunk off your head, shift
from your chest so you stand
taller and skip some.

A school of fish swims
hard left then hard right
inside you, all point
the same way at the same time,
making you smile, making you lean
toward me on our walk to the park.

I pretend I don't see them,
smirk, step from the path
to walk the hill. We reach
the garden at dusk; small lamps dot
the grass, form a mirror of the night sky.

I feel you stagger a bit,
see you grin slipping
your arm through mine, and wonder
what kind of fish they are, how big
their school is, how much room they use
to whirl about within you.

I stare at the house every time I drive by
after D. A. Powell

you'd want to go down Evaline Street with them;   see
who'd changed their mind. who has lines under their eyes. see

who has the crazies at their feet and listen
to the songs we would get off on: someone will be spinning.

you'd want to drive by the stop sign that exists
because the girls were struck there. luckily they lived.

not time for them to sit with our Joey,
only dead a few months.   our aching still abundant.

he'd wear a tiara: strength of royalty.
a setting in his curls.   a protective shield.

what was it that was so good?
catnip, pair of socks, queen alien, hand rolled, back porch.

ten-day eviction notice: jobs abandoned to drive nights
singing into sunrise rush hour.   smoking and laughing.

faces out the window fluttering: stared–at
car bouncing its tires through the steep streets;

McArdle and Beechwood.   Boggs and Monitor.
getting schooled on motion. unveiled.

people painted together.   people painted shut.
people embedded within each other: breathing through
the bubbles.

there were cracks when they dried. you chipped
yourself to taste.   Virgin Mary blue

couldn't drive far enough.   the car getting smaller.
everyone was spilling out the doors.

Hedging

This dentist will go into my mouth
without knowing that in my head
is your mom's cancer, & in my gut a fibroid
the size of my open hand waiting to be cut out,
& back home are kind prayers
from the family who aren't sure
if we're a couple, but they know
to pray when people are scared,
& they know I love, no matter how,
& I'll hear Franz Ferdinand's "Take
Me Out" over & over knowing it will
stamp this summer somehow, & I'll
never be able to forget the fear
underlining this stark wet July every
time I hear it, & the shrub I've parked
in front of here at the dentist's office
is the kind I've been picking at my whole life,
the snapped-off branch soft & ordinary, evergreen
boxwood bristle still hollowed in my fist
as I steer back to you tonguing the tender hole
where my worn-down tooth used to be.

Grief or *She took it hard*

If she takes it, then it can't
drag her dirt-eclipsed fingernails
backward into some moonlit cave
and plant orchards of unease inside
the tiny pores of her stomach.

       The tall ache of the gut-pines creak.

Lying still in scratchy sheets,
she lets silence suck through her ear,
heartbeats jackhammering into her
flimsy pillow, its stained yellow rings
rippling around her head like a halo,
like a long-ago phone call.

five

Electric Grasshoppers

If I were small enough
to sit inside the grooves
of green paint racing down
my wall, small enough to lie
down within the indent made
by the paintbrush standing
on course bristles, then
I'd whistle, if I was up to it,
or hum, if I felt like it, otherwise
I might be mistaken for some
fast scratch, chip or crack.
I know I'd sleep and surely
dream of giant boulders dropped
from great heights, bursting open,
erupting electric grasshoppers
in every possible direction.

Reassurances

Listen to Whitney Houston
ask "How will I know?"
like it's still summer of '85,
while outside you will hear
an upset dog barking
out of fear of another dog
also barking out of fear
as their leashes both pull
taut in the cacophony
that startles us all,
launching robins
into the pink sky
of this frozen and otherwise
still morning.

A woman's voice:
It's okay! It's okay!
trying to reassure everyone,
but her pitch is hinged too high,
too bright, and although
the dogs soon settle
into defensive huffing
stretched all the way out
to the end of their leashes,
no one really believes her.

Missed Call

The potato's eyes turned bright green, stark tiny cacti to
whom I gave no time, before snapping off, shaking nubs in
my fist like rattling dice.

Luck or not, a woman on my voicemail:
Hey Margie—I just wanteda'tell ya:
the fish I was thinkin' about was anchovies—OK?

Anchovies are like eating an eyebrow, Eddie Murphy said,
& I wasn't going to eat the potato either,

but it sat on the rack scattered with fat bright eyes.
I couldn't leave it alone.
When Margie's friend called,
I was standing in the kitchen suspicious

of her unknown number blinking on my phone,
buds still clutched in my hand.
Her voice a soft-faced neighbor with granddogs who warns

about black ice the minute it gets chilly.
I thought about calling her back,
going to sit in her kitchen, drink Sanka
& smoke Pall Malls, eat unpopular cookies

while we tsk & shrug around her table with *Jeopardy!*
in the background. Later, in a parking garage,
I pulled keys from my pocket and found

the bitty potato fingers caught between them.
I thought of little fish right then,
& Margie on a rotary, recipes stashed in a metal drawer.
From the 7th floor, I flicked each eye

over the railing into the downtown street,
too dark to see them fall far,
each eye more or less like the snow that was falling with it.

Hard Like a Stud

How many are naked in windows
overlooking the city from high posh boxes,
naked to no one except the skyline of Pittsburgh,
her watery legs spreading all around us as I climb
McArdle again, that street I once rode slanted-up
packed in the Honda—all of us—my head tilted out/
same angle of tree line that soon breaks
to downtown's whole blinking mouthful shushing
across the river. I push myself to remember wetness
windblown from my eyes; the reckless joy.
The moon so full my clit's hard like a stud
and these people are walking past the moon
somehow, not looking at her, not looking at the guy
in the condo above them either, full-frontal,
his shadowy dick nosing away from the cold glass.

Work Drinks

While you are dropkicking
your husband's boat
into conversation
about your deliberate cool
hair, you spill your IPA and say *fuck*
without committing to it.
>I'm wobbling a little
>with margaritas in me almost
>hoping for a lack of resentment
>and a needlepoint pillow
>stitched by Dame Judi Dench
>that says *You're a twat* on it.

When You Walk Away from the Campsite as It's Getting Dark

You can come back now, I'll say
& mean it deeply, even though
I can still see your back through the trees,
shoulder blades realigning in shadows
as you hunt for kindling, your red shirt
fading into forest dusk,
because who are you or I
without our lips popping open
just beyond a long, cold drink,
without our house framing anything,
everything escapable and burning quick
bright dots high into the air,
straight through to the darkness of what surrounds us,
which is really just another way to say *sky* & what it contains.

Kids Out the Window

sound like goats,
the sky gray, like the lining
of my pockets, smells wet
like my McDonald's birthday
party—how I loved
the fryer, the behind-
the-scenes, the candied
Grimace on my cake
too sweet but gritty
between my teeth,
which are rotting early—
a constant ache in my mouth,
a little guy with a pickaxe
beneath my molars heaving
its point into my gums: he must
be installing steel tracks
inside my jawline for some subterranean
city that will never be unearthed
when I smile—no one can see it,
and it's likely that I'll never point
this out to you: I'll just watch
a woodpecker peck the awning
outside my window without
welcoming it into my mouth.
I'll try not to worry
about what's beneath your gumline—

what hover-tracked universe you harbor
inside your skull, and instead
I'll think about goats and how
they kick everything over, and
so would I if I could get away with it.

six

Spaced

I hear the stars are twenty
million million miles apart
something like my eyes
each suspended in a vitreous
harbor for floating specks
      passing comets
      the bending light
      of my gravitational lens

From Crown Down beyond Her

My neighbor is showering
through these Kennedy-era
walls: the skidding whistle
of old pipes will last fifteen
minutes or so: she's scrubbing
herself just on the other side
of my cold wall, maybe just
standing there, biblical,
like I often do, hands cupped
to catch water at her chest,
chin tilted like a statue
of Mary perched on a shelf.
Surely there's redness
patching her skin as she dials
higher & higher for warmth,
inching the knob to keep the hot sting,
letting the water butter her
from crown down beyond her
into the drain, muting her ears,
water-beard falling
from around her open mouth.

Lighthouse Mouth

Green Pipe, you are not some squirrel
standing a gentle G stance on the wide lawn.
You pop from the wet cold dirt a curve.

A kicked top lip cracked, smashed.
A cleft palate. A spidery string
of webbed leaves: your uvula.

I could fist your face, tip my head
into your hole, scrape my nose
on your cracked green lips.

Cricket in your throat. Legs shaking
in your cold vocal tube. Echo at dark:
cricket in your guttural golf-ball cup.

If I crawled down into you, I'd call to myself
through the pipeline, an old-fashioned wire,
yelling letters spackled into one whole sound:

my name, a dirt-smeared lighthouse mouth filled with barking,
howling the open range with the ache of the lean forward.

Heath Ledger Is Dead

after O'Hara

Work over   I'm stopping for a sixer
WILKES BAR   Jancey Street   Pittsburgh 2008
it is 5:00 and the bar is filling with Yinzers
who squint at me when I open the door
letting sunlight
into the   smoke hole.

I lean my dirty sleeves on the bar between an older man
whose pants are covered in white paint splotches
and a guy wearing a jumpsuit   MORNINGSIDE AUTO
on the back.

                    The bartender gets up
from his Bud Light behind the poker machine
and points   (doesn't
talk to anyone) with the long ash
of his Benson and Hedges and I say IRON CITY
SIX PACK PLEASE at the same moment I see
on the TV in the corner Heath took too many pills
I smack my hand on the bar in amazement
no one   looks up so I hand the guy a five
and four ones then go next door to the RITE AID
to buy body wash and mint gum
but they don't have the mint I want so I get cinnamon
     a change of flavor would be nice
     the Joker in *The Dark Knight*
is horribly satisfying and the tent scene in *Brokeback Mountain*
is masturbation material for sure and I'm jealous that anyone

gets to kiss Shannyn Sossamon
ever   for real or not   I buy THE POST-GAZETTE
from the bitter cashier
before I walk down Chislett
and pop into STAGNOS Bakery
where I ask the stich n'sew woman behind the donut counter
for a sausage roll
pay for my San Pellegrino with the 10 I found in the parking
lot at work   I'm thinking of the handful
of male actors I would actually have sex with
and he's near the top of

                                        that short list
because he doesn't seem douche-y   just tuned-in
and when I go outside
it's late day or early evening
                 I am unsettled by the abrupt disappearance
of people and walking down the sidewalk I'm grateful for
butt sex because it's another way to get into people who can
be so very hard to get into.

Oh, Grate

Like I could leave you
sniffling in the corner
of the room   your hot
breath marking my body
with some tainted gesture
I breathe out   I could bust out
the window or stick my body
halfway up the wall   spider myself wide
pop out ribbons & firecrackers
from kaleidoscopic holes in my head

You & your salty depths
your hole to my own unending   I've dropped Matchbox
cars into you: little yellow Trans Am
with the bashed front end   blue Hemi Cuda convertible
the tiny ambulance coming in you
with its antennae bitten down to stub   Even
the VW Rabbit teetered on your slanted edge
then down into your tin it went
Talk to me
Cough something up for Christ's sake
It's ridiculous out here

Dinner Party. Oh.

Table for twelve & I am moved
to remove my shoes, slip–
slide my body down the front of my chair.
Knees reach the floor, & I'm eye to bean
with green bean almondine.

No one seems to notice. So I duck my head
below, crawl to the center of the table,
caged in by feet & knees of people I know
but have never seen this way.

My eye to the y of each crotch, where panty hamsters
& ball sacs are tucked behind shifty skirts & suit pants.

If Greg were here, this would be our spacecraft.
The nuts & bolts, our controls.
We'd drive these loose legs right out the front
window, above streetlamps
& into the inky, dappled sky where it's cool.
Where we could actually breathe.

But underneath I hear banter muted. I can see
who's touching who under the table. I know
by the tapping of toes who's ready to go.

Cook Forest Ghosts

No roof or window for filter,
just sunlight pinching over
a crowd of trees, & here is coffee
steeped on the fire, & here is *Against Which*
resting on a log in the cool-strike breeze
grazing my open neck. Here is Michelle
in blues & sturdy earrings spelling *pall* or *pal*
in a notebook over the wicked
afternoon glare. Nearby, the squeak-
voiced teenager saves a coupon
for fifty cents from burning
in their pit—his father says:
a babushka is a scarf worn on your head.
There's polka from their radio all day long
like a Pennsylvania fire-hall wedding out here.
Continual horseshoes
clang into the cold night
until, after some sleep, I slip
out of our tent, stoop on the tops
of my boots in the wet brush,
bristling silence, crouching in the steel
light beaming between branches
& make ghosts with my mouth in the chill.

Saleslady

Saleslady hair is purest
in the spongy light
of the bathroom mirror after
coffee, after clanking her spoon
around in her bowl of whatever.
And her barrette kills me
from above her ear
when I see it glimmer later,
holding back her vague curls
as she tries to sell me nothing
I care for—that silverness stabs
quick at my eyes,
which implode
with tenderness for her,
for the way she gets ready
in the morning—how we all
get ready in the morning,
putting ourselves together,
combing our hair, looking
into our own eyes
and taking a last look
before leaving.

"I've Got Walls for Days" contains the song title "Bells for Her" from Tori Amos's album *Under the Pink.*

"Evacuate My Brain" contains the lyrics "honey bring it close to my lips" which is from Armand Van Helden's remix of Tori Amos's song "Professional Widow." This poem also contains the lyrics "call on me—spin spin sugar"; crawl on me—spin spin sugar"; and "twist on me—spin spin sugar," all of which come from the song "Spin Spin Sugar" by Sneaker Pimps.

"Cook Forest Ghosts" mentions Ross Gay's book *Against Which.*

"Crocuses, Baby" is for Michelle Stoner.

ACKNOWLEDGMENTS

Grateful acknowledgment to the journals where the
following poems, sometimes in earlier versions and with
earlier titles, first appeared:

- *2 Bridges Review*: "Oh, Grate"
- *5AM*: "Night on Rattlesnake Hill"
- *BLOOM*: "No Better"
- *Burnside Review*: "Tennessee Bourbon"
- *City Paper*: "From Crown Down Beyond Her,"
  "Red Dot"
- *Girls with Glasses*: "On Boggs Avenue"
- *Pittsburgh Quarterly*: "Evacuate My Brain," "Stripper
  Karaoke: One Dollar Well Drinks," "Crocuses, Baby"
- *Tupelo Quarterly*: "Kids Out the Window"
- *Voices from the Attic Vol. XVI–XXI*: "Burning Rubber,"
  "Scoring the Sunlit Halves & Thirds," "Calling into
  the Grate," "Domenic Whipped a Palm—,"
  "Smashing the Inch"

I'm wild with gratitude for each person mentioned here,
and for many I have not mentioned. I have multiple secret
appreciations.

Special thanks to all who have encouraged me along the
way: in the Carlow University parking lot after Madwomen
in the Attic sessions; in private workshops; after readings;
under the trees and in workshops at Drew University; in
other conversations that have stuck with me to this day. I

know who are, and your words are incredibly important to me. If you're still alive, I thank you directly. And if you're not, I thank you indirectly.

Absolute mountainous thanks to Jan Beatty – so many things spinning in this orbit wouldn't have spun without your stellar guidance, sage insights, and cosmic currents.

Enormous gratitude to Judith Vollmer for your universe of wisdom and for opening all kinds of colorful portals in my existence.

Heartfelt appreciation to my mentors, and to teachers who have brought me (and these poems) to places I never would have expected: Michael Dennison, Patricia Dobler, Ross Gay, Aracelis Girmay, Sigrid King, Joan Larkin, Anne Marie Macari, Jane Mead, Mihaela Moscaliuc, Alicia Ostriker, Patrick Rosal, Ira Sadoff, Gerald Stern, Jean Valentine, Stacey Waite, Michael Waters, Ellen Doré Watson, and Bruce Weigl.

Profound gratitude to Cara Armstrong, Tess Barry, Jennifer Jackson Berry, Amber Coppings, Marisa Frasca, Roberto Carlos Garcia, Darla Himeles, Gail Langstroth, Hattie Jo Lehman, Yesenia Montilla, Lynne McEniry, Rachel Mennies, Emily Mohn-Slate, Stacie Prettiman, Anne Rashid, Kayla Sargeson, Heidi Sheridan, Adam Shreckhise, Bernadette Ulsamer, Lori Wilson, Michael Wargula, and

Joseph Yatsko. Each of you is important to me and my work in varied and unspeakable ways, and I appreciate you more than I can say.

Immense thanks to everyone at Get Fresh Books for making all of this possible especially Roberto Carlos Garcia.

True gratitude, too, to the folks of the Madwomen in the Attic Creative Writing Workshops, the Drew University MFA Program in Poetry and Poetry in Translation, and the Pittsburgh poetry community. These are magical universes filled with magical people, and I couldn't be more grateful for the opportunity to be among you.

Special thanks to artist Liz Nichtberger for use of her "Misty Day" painting on the cover.

Soft-hearted love, too, to Madi, Livy, and Leo whose pawprints and purrs are all over these pages. Little anchors.

Indescribable thanks to my family for loving and supporting me, most especially my mother and father – I'm lucky because of you.

And most expressly to Michelle for all the colors and all the lights – my appreciation is lit in every direction for you.